THE SHADOW LIST

JEN SOOKFONG LEE

POEMS

Also by
JEN
SOOKFONG LEE

FICTION
The Better Mother
The Conjoined
The End of East

NON-FICTION
Gentlemen of the Shade
Whatever Gets You Through

CHILDREN
The Animals of Chinese New Year
Chinese New Year
Finding Home
Shelter

THE SHADOW LIST

POEMS

JEN SOOKFONG LEE

A Buckrider Book

Buckrider Books is an imprint of Wolsak and Wynn Publishers.

Editor: Paul Vermeersch | Copy editor: Ashley Hisson
Cover and interior design: Kilby Smith-McGregor
Author photograph: Kyrani Karavanos
Typeset in Adobe Caslon Pro, MedPen and Verveine
Printed by Coach House Printing Company Toronto, Canada

10 9 8 7 6 5 4 3 2 1

  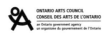

The publisher gratefully acknowledges the support of the Ontario Arts Council, the Canada Council for the Arts and the Government of Canada.

Buckrider Books
280 James Street North
Hamilton, ON
Canada L8R 2L3

Library and Archives Canada Cataloguing in Publication

Title: The shadow list : poems / Jen Sookfong Lee.
Names: Lee, Jen Sookfong, author.
Identifiers: Canadiana 2020040976X | ISBN 9781989496282 (softcover)
Classification: LCC PS8623.E442 S53 2021 | DDC C811/.6—dc23

For ANDREA,
        CAROLYN
and CARRIE

CONTENTS

PART THREE

ACKNOWLEDGEMENTS

INTRODUCTION

This is what you'll need to understand:

Cameron Crowe is to blame for everything.
Sunshine is an insult.
You may never learn to swim but so what?
A dog is the love of your life.
The pretty poems are dead inside.

*

The books are the only things you have left
behind that make sentence-by-sentence sense. You think,
Hearts break all the time, but that doesn't come close
to explaining away the vomit in the toilet from crying
then drinking and then crying again,

or the bone-deep certainty that, when this ends,
people will say, *She was full of life, a loving friend*,
when you know it's only half-true or maybe not even.
You deserve punishment, self-inflicted or otherwise.

                                                                *

The hearts you break matter less and less (this is a lie, see above).
Your greatest worry is that your son
will grow up to be just like you.
Laundry doesn't fold itself.
You still don't know what *doubling down* means.

✱

You can shout anything you want
through the open windows: warnings, spells, limericks.
The wind will suck it all up, turn every wish or curse
meaningless as they are blown into fragments, hurled
against power lines and trees dying from the tops down.

There is a purpose to this, of course: it is the act
of casting them outward, of yelling so loudly that your
body caves inward with the effort, your abdominals
hard as stone for the first time ever.

This is necessary.

Without it, you would stay soft and silent, curled
like a baby mouse in holes too small for a human thumb.

*

Protect your child, even though you know you can't.
Being smarter hasn't helped much.
Stand up straight.

*

So you will always try. There is no alternative, is there?
You can beat at winter for weeks and weeks
and spring will eventually arrive and you can trick
yourself into believing it came for you.

The sharp tips of crocuses, the dawn, the thickening light,
all because you called them into being with your rage,
with the furious living you did in the winter dark

(mascara like ashes, satin
underwear, unfamiliar musk in your hair and mouth).

This violence, this volume
is how you will try to change what seems like fate.

*

Fearing the outdoors keeps people alive.
Never trust the man in the long coat.

*

Tread softly, your friends say. *Be quiet.*
And you laugh because you have heard
this your whole life, even as you cracked
your knuckles and hurled your phone
into a public street and combed last night's
sweat through your hair with grubby hands.

Writers are supposed to be introverts.
And you laugh even harder.

*

The hurt will fuck you up
but you will appear fine and this,
above all else, is your gift.

PART ONE

RIDER

1. Fake leather pants
2. That sticky table under the only good light in this bar
3. The left turn, never the right
4. Lipstick: red-red like the first pinpricks of blood
5. Dill pickle chips
6. Your mother's phone calls (which you ignore)
7. Orange juice in the morning
8. Coffee in the morning
9. If possible, sex in the morning
10. The last doughnut/croissant/cupcake because you always get yours

INFESTATION

In the kitchen, they hang upside down on the ceiling,
wings folded, their bodies tucked like arrowheads,
antennae quivering so slightly you have to stand
on a chair and squint to see any movement at all.

In the bedroom at night, they fly around
your reading lamp and you can hear
their exoskeletons singe on the hot light bulb
as you open book after book without finishing any.

You burrow deep in your closet, looking for abandoned
cocoons in your sweater pile, open every container
in your pantry until you find larvae in the quinoa.
You swear they are pulsating, like they already

know how to breathe. *It figures*, you think, *trying to eat
healthy results in a plague.* Steel cut oats, pearled barley,
brown rice. All in their clear containers, so they can judge
you from within. You compost them, without regret.

The traps emit pheromones. You stay up
half the night, watching the moths circle the trap
that smells like sex, the trap that will lure them in
with the heady scent of moth desire.

They will fly in, land on the adhesive and never escape.
They last four, maybe five days before they stop
struggling and die, their tiny moth feet covered
in an unforgiving glue. This satisfies you.

Where they have come from, you don't know,
but you create an origin story in your head.
The elderly Chinese couple next door, you think, *it must be them.*
Maybe they keep dry goods in their bedroom, drywall

the only thing separating your headboard from theirs.
You remember that time you cleaned out your mother's house
and found a dozen bottles of soy sauce and seven packages
of dried cloud ear fungus hidden behind the coats in the closet.

What if there is a shelf of mung beans and jasmine rice
right behind your pillows? There the moths
build cocoons, hatch and then fly off
into your open window, straight toward your bedside lamp.

The moths know.
This is why they have come to you,
toward the only light in a dark building,
toward the promise of sex and a long, sticky death.

They know you read at night.
They know you are alone.
They know you itch with loneliness until you could scream
so you read and fail until you fall asleep.

A SCIENTIFIC TREATISE

I

Carbon dating
Dendrochronology
The Minkowski metric

Time building like dust on shelves.
Time coating your mouth after too much sangria.
Time and your son is just like you, weeping from anxiety.

This is your version of science.

2

It's winter now.
Cars spin their wheels on layers of ice,
each forming with every subsequent Arctic front:
three days, four days, eight days later.
Overhead, a branch on the bigleaf maple
is cracking under the weight of snow
that has melted and refrozen
like pyrite gone silver.

3

If the half-life of uranium is 4.5 billion years, how long
does it take for feelings to divide in half and then half again,
reduced to nano-dust that you feel only if you stand
alone, eyes closed, in the smallest room, breath paused?

Everything else changes. Paint on the walls fade.
The dog hops, tentative and arthritic, down the stairs,
her body newly angled to the right. Even you.

The synovium in your feet swell in the shower. When you slip
on black ice, you scream and this fear is the final way you will age.

HOW THE WINTER CHANGES YOU

Morning and nothing will melt today. You stay
as still as the frost that now coats your windows,
white on glass, you in white sheets.
It grows inward, that cold, in fractures thin as threads

until your blood is half-crystalline and brittle,
and the cracks spider all the way around.
There you are, felled by an ache
because your heart might be split in two.

You know it's morning when you hear
the truck tires on the iced-over puddles in the alley,
the cranes groaning as they swing
above the snowy construction site behind your little house.

It feels final, doesn't it?
Giving up movement, heat, lunch with friends,
the solid warmth of a cock in your mouth. Maybe
this is your version of Lent, virtue via numbness.

You salted your front steps the night before. For what?
You're not leaving again. The stairs
could have been an ice moat, three feet wide, slippery as fuck,
separating you from everything else.

You panic at the idea of someone dropping
by and finding you like this, hidden
in your dawn-bright bedroom, mulling, slowly freezing.
But then you remember it's just a waiting game.

Imagine if all the sinners knew your secret.
They would run toward the ocean on New Year's Day,
bare feet flying over the hardened sand.
They would be the ones left behind, adamant

in the water, pink and brown skin
giving way to blue, waiting to feel innocent again.
Assholes and sociopaths, frozen in the sea.
Until spring anyway.

Eventually the salt will blow away or be licked clean
by those skinny, shivering raccoons who walk
through the courtyard every morning at dawn
and the ice will grow again, impassable.

FIVE BREAKUPS
WITH THE SAME MAN

You sent him a very long text,
the kind you have to tap twice to read.
He didn't respond. It was Christmas.

.

During sex, he said he loved you.
You pretended not to hear him, went home,
and he didn't call for six months.

.

He met you at a bar. You had to call
him the next day, standing in the lobby
of your friend's apartment building
in a coat that still carried his cologne
and say you couldn't see him again.
But you did. Three weeks later.

.

He called.
He said he could be a stepfather to your son.
And your tears were vicious and hot but still.
You said no and he said he would walk away.

.

In an email, he asked for a poem
you had written about him.
You sent it. He didn't write back.
What did you expect.

TEXT ETIQUETTE

You think how men's bellies are their most vulnerable parts.
It's the slack skin, the way the muscles are so easily softened
when they forget to clench early in the day, or when they're
just about to come. It's a punishment, wanting to see this now.

> You deserve it.
> After all, it was you
> who kept those ugly secrets.
> You know the ones.

In the night, when your child
is asleep in the next room, you write
text messages in the dark. It seems fitting,
poetic even, to write six words or sometimes twelve

and send them with a velocity
that applies only to molecules
and pixelated language, broken

by your phone into syllables
and then letters and then a fine
digital dust carried by a digital wind.

It has been fourteen minutes.
Your phone blinks its blue light.

It could be the man who carried
your crying son home in the snow.
It could be your friend
whose husband just left her.
It could be your mother, sending
a photograph that is a square of black
but for the fleshy blur in the bottom
right corner that you are sure is her thumb.

It could be the other man, the one
you've been expecting to come back to you.

This bedroom was designed for you alone. That wallpaper,
silvery in all lights. The sheer white curtains, hung in a knot
you retie every week. The queen bed where you lie in the middle,
arms and legs in a sprawl. Those invited are never permanent.

You curl up and turn away
from the phone
on your nightstand. The messages
chirp but you can sleep through it.
You'll get to them in the morning.

COMMUNITY GARDEN

There, the bolting black kale,
taller than it has any right to be
and not the twitter troll who asked
if you were on your period.

In the corner, a pile of dead
zucchini leaves, spotted with rot
and not the neighbour who yelled
at you about a parking stall.

Lining the sidewalk, invasive
creeping charlie and not
your mother complimenting
your ex-husband's new wife.

THIRD PERSON INTIMATE

Your poor protagonist, face up
to watch the meteor shower symbolically
arcing across the August sky.
She never really had a chance.

You are used to writing novels,
to placing a human in the middle
of a slowly unwinding nighttime dilemma,
darkness hiding her indecisive, rock-heavy feet.

Your psychologist would say, *You write
the choices you're afraid to make.* The women
in your books are bad mothers. They leave
their children, sit with regret in their lap

as if it were an overfed cat sharpening its claws
on the arm of the living room chair. They leave, rent
small apartments where silence is everywhere, like mould.
You have never. You would never. And yet.

THE WHITE LIE

Don't worry, you say, *I will never write about you.*

As proof, you offer, *I never write*
about my marriage. What a half-truth that is.
Your old marriage runs like an underground river
through everything: those poems, the ones with
trees rotting from the inside out, or the cracks
that secretly spiderwebbed through your body
until they broke you open and you shivered
in the new, January air.

In your bedroom, the lamp
with the gold shade casts
the magic light that seems accidental
but never was. You want the men
hovering above you to look soft,
their edges furred as if they might
love you enough to text you back.

You touch his beard, your fingertips
trailing over his jaw. If you could, you would
rest your head in that hollow of his neck,
and you would stay there through morning
and nightmares, through a summer thunderstorm,
through a cloud of killer bees. That beard.
You could promise him everything.

You said you wouldn't write about him.
You might have meant it then, when his mouth
lingered on your ear because he knew you liked
the whisper. You would have agreed to anything:
more children, a cat, his mother in the laneway
house out back. You don't ask yourself the hard
questions about confinement, rage, escape.

And if he asks? It's simple. You will stop, look
at the shadows pulsing like breath on the pebbled
white ceiling and lie.

PLAYLIST
for Harry Styles

In your dream, Harry Styles is singing to you, mournfully,

and you think he might kiss you, notes and tongue
in your mouth simultaneously. You touch the sleeve
of his brocade jacket, stiff with silk threads
stitched into chrysanthemums.

When you roll over, your half-awake brain
remembers that playlist a man made for you as a joke,
a playlist designed to mock your love of sappy pop ballads.
The Lumineers and Mumford, Vanessa Carlton and Lisa Loeb,
that one song by Gord Downie about divorce and the ocean.

Your alarm clock glows red. 2:36 a.m.

You sit up. The speakers in your house
have come on in the middle of the night
and are playing sad Cyndi Lauper.
Outside, you hear a car door slam.

He was standing outside, wasn't he, on your deck,
close enough to connect to your Wi-Fi,
his face lit up by his phone.

Now it's Culture Club and you don't
know if the hurt is meant for Boy George or you.

His face would have glowed green in the dark
as he scrolled through your saved music and chose
these songs. Precisely these.

✷

The inside of your little house is intimate knowledge. Here,
he brought you coffee in the morning. He installed a dimmer
for your dining room light that, afterward, sparked and singed
the drywall. When he pushed you face down on the bed

and you crawled away, crying, he ignored your texts
for eighteen hours and you thought it was fine,
you could be done, but then he came back
and you made him spaghetti and meatballs.

His head hung low and you thought, *Okay, I guess.*

✶

If he thinks about it, he will know where you are sitting
right now, back against the headboard, eyes on the curtained
window, listening to the wind, the traffic on Hastings,
a falling dumpster lid. You listen to everything,

waiting for him to pound the door down, to hiss
that you are a fucking coward, to spit the words he wrote
in letter after letter, to tie you to the bed with the chain he keeps
in his nightstand, or the sound of his car driving into the back gate,

over and over again. You wait.
Your son coughs in his sleep and that's your heart jumping.
Fuck that thing. Fuck your unreliable heart.

An hour later, you creep to the window and pull
the curtain back three inches. Everything is still.
No wind. No traffic. No voices bickering in the alley

behind the hotel bar. You pull the router
from the wall and there is no electric hum now either.

You haven't seen this man in five months, but he may as well
be in the room, whispering that you are a cumslut,
that your pussy needs him.

He never yelled. As if that made a difference.

PART TWO

YESTERDAY, YOU HAD THE BEST OF INTENTIONS

A glass of water, tepid and undrunk, in the bedroom air.
A body beside you whose movements are so small
and so slow you cannot measure them.
Muddy, thick hours spent listening to the night pass.

This is the long rolling of time, that liquid dim
that breaks over the neighbours' rooftops and leaks
through a crack in those curtains you have never hemmed.
The broken lamp beside the garage buzzing, a raccoon

walking upside down, claws tapping and tapping
on the gutter it clings to. You squint, the continued
watch in the night. The black hurts your eyes.
Do you know what you're watching for?

There are secrets, indecent and jagged like a stranger's teeth
biting the thin line of your clavicle. You could whisper
them now and he would not hear you. But no.
You should wait. Nighttime lulls. That soft, enabling dark.

Outside, the first chickadee sings.
You have twenty minutes, maybe thirty,
before the sky lifts, burning, and kills
what you have been staring at all night long.

TORNADO

This – the deserted sidewalk with only your feet, the dark
that exists because you do too – is what you asked for.
This city where asphalt is streaked with long stripes

of blood or shit or mud. Here, you step
into the January wind because it hurts, because it drills
into the skin on your face and the hard pain is good.

Behind you is the house you have just left.
It was once yours, a house you helped rebuild, painting
shingles one by one. It grew outward and you stayed inside,

behind the walls that drew the sea-salted air in,
blew the spoiled, angry air out. *Your house breathes*, the architect
once said, but the goosebumps on your arms already knew.

You walk, past the grass the crows have turned over
looking for grubs, past the apartment building crumbling
under decayed hanging baskets and empties and mould.

You could whisper at the Christmas lights still hanging
from balconies, *This is where I'm going, you will find me*, but you don't.
The wind is in your mouth now anyway, a cyclone.

You were born right over there.
You know where to turn, where the skinniest shadows
unroll across an alley. The silence of this city at night.

When you were younger, you walked toward the water
and no one knew. It was easy to sneak away and head
north and north again until there was nothing but the port

to your left and a rocky beach that tore the soles of your shoes
before you even reached the water. It was easy here,
among the Styrofoam cups and pieces of glass too small

to pick up but still beautiful. This city. You hated it then.
You could imagine yourself in another city,
by another ocean, in new clothes that fit a curvier body.

There is no silence, really. There is the ocean.
The seagulls circling and circling.
That wind. And you.

For the last seventeen years, you have been talking of pawnshops,
open dumpsters and the chain-link fences with human-sized holes
torn through their middles. Better to have smiled and said,

I dreamed of you, we should get a cat, I actually love the rain.

It's true: The lights are what people want to remember.
Not the gaps between brick buildings, not the stairs that lead
to tunnels beneath the streets. Not the bodies under awnings.

Only you will remember. You stop on the hill and look down
at the old concrete treads in the sidewalk. They lead west,
a grey brick road. So you walk because you have nowhere else to be.

WHEN YOU READ HIS POEMS

It's a sliver of your body in the middle of a line, embedded,
half-obscured with other words: glass, the knife edges of paper, sirens.
That's you, and you know it.

You tell yourself: You are bigger than that. It's only poetry and slight.
It's not your weight on his chest, both of you damp and swollen
with August heat. It's not a photograph, well lit and unforgiving.

Not even your voice in his head when he remembers that phone call
at three in the morning when you were both drunk and looking for sex.
Just a poem. Like this.

✻

You remind yourself: He wasn't the first. There were the boys
who wrote to compete with you, or the boys who wrote songs
they sung in your mother's basement and you thought you might die

because your heart ran with the chords and then stopped, abrupt.
If you looked now, you could find the right box. Inside: a single dog tag,
letters from Israel, Taiwan, Australia, small-town Ontario.

You had sorted the piles, labelled them *office: miscellaneous*, so you,
huddled in a hoodie and your girlhood quilt, could read them in the night
for years to come. A sleepless secret. Quiet, you thought, and harmless.

*

You have seen ghosts before, hovering transparently
in front of photographs, double selves in low light. Your face
in words when the words are not yours: a ghost in a funhouse mirror.

You cannot stop him from writing the shake of your body
when it folded and levelled. Would he, if you asked? You know the answer
as well as you know the soft hair in the small of his back

or the dip in his shoulder that you thought
– hysterically, briefly – had been dented just for you.
You know. And so does he. You would never ask.

WISHES

There is a stray eyelash on your cheek. You pick it off,
balance it on your finger, close your eyes and blow.
So. What do you wish for?

Babies,
an A-frame cabin on a cliff above the white-edged ocean,
the skin you had when you were twenty-five,
rain on your bare arms,
a room filled with helium balloons,
a cat, long-haired and suspicious.

No, of course not. There is a shadow list, one saved
in your head where its grime is obscured by work
and sandwiches and the weather tomorrow.

You want to run the first kiss
and the eleventh kiss
and the last kiss
through his head,
parsing each breath and
lazy, stuttered beat because he
is just so manic with longing.

You want a dog who hates everyone but you.
A car that makes noises that sound like sex.
You want to know what your pubic hair is supposed to look like.
You want a newspaper just for the horoscopes.
Pork rinds.
A short leather skirt that pulls across your ass.

Naked whispers at dawn, French toast with strawberries,
lemon verbena hand cream. That was you, for a while,
in a green house on a nice street where blue jays sang, perched
in the maple trees, and you wondered who was screaming.

The eyelash is gone. You imagine it floating through dust and fruit flies,
watching for married men on business trips or young men
who will never guess your real age. It will land, eventually, someplace
dirty and limp with a saturated damp that cannot be described.

BUT THE MUSCLE MEMORY

I

In a room with only one window, the wind blows in
leaves that fall from the city trees. They're dotted
with rot from the rain you have just run through
in ill-advised heels, afraid you would lose your nerve.

Two hours later, you measure his torso and count
four hand spans across. He seems an unbreakable mass.
Here is a man who says you're smart when he kisses you,

the edges of your longwear lipstick like scalpels
in their precision. This isn't a surprise. After all, stripped
of the bra and mascara and earrings, you're only just pretty enough.

Smart, he says again, rolling
open the window so wide
a second man could walk in,
naked, slick with rain, tall.

2

In grade nine you wrote in your diary, *I hate my face,*
and meant it. There was the oversized green jean jacket,
the steel-toed boots, the plastic bin of toques beside the bed.
Then you had supposed that you were hiding.

Now you know that the truth was more sinister
than that. You were burying yourself,
the not-yet-pretty version, hoping she
would suffocate, shrink under the weight and die.

In the summers, you took the bus by yourself to English Bay
and walked the seawall until you found the right rock, the one
that cut into the ocean, flat on top and narrow. Here you sat.
The sun might have burned your face clean off.

Years later, you forgot. There were jobs, a marriage,
the apartment downtown on the sixth floor. You learned
that your mouth was your best feature and that your bony hips
could be hidden by the right dresses, if the lighting was good.

3

When your son was born, your midwife showed you
the placenta, double-lobed and the red of muscles
that expand, contract and remember.
There may have been a twin, she said.

They grow and then disappear, leaving only the barest evidence.
Some extra blood. The oversized placenta that the nurses
took pictures of, just in case. It's genetic:
the desire to destroy the seemingly weaker one.

Your son on your chest and you are defenseless, skin stretched
so thin old wounds pulse behind the new ones
you have not yet catalogued. Look: your old face
and straight-angled body. But then your son's first cry and you forget again.

4

That is, until this night. The air rushes in through that one
wide window as that man's wide hands undress you, a different,
colder wind you recognize from the chafe on your skin,
for the way it scrapes at you until you are brittle and sore

and ready to splinter into pieces like cheap plastic diamonds.
It's the pre-frost that will soon crystallize into black ice on pavement.
You don't have long before winter creeps in.
Three weeks, a month if you're lucky.

Now you know: Your old self never died.
Untended, she grew, unfurling sideways
under your uneventful, grown-up life.
Funny how that happens.

In this room, with this man, she emerges,
hungry and mad for air, and he is taking the credit.
There you are, he says. *I knew it.* His voice
is lost in the all the commotion, but you don't care.

5

You smell salt. Yours and his.
From the almonds still on the table,
from the mud-ringed inlet two blocks away.
There is nowhere, you think, *this city doesn't intrude.*

Nowhere it hasn't been:
on your body, in that room, as smell or wind
between new-old, delirious you and the man
you are running your tongue along, inch by square inch.

Jaw slack and ass up, nothing
you're doing is pretty anymore.
You eat, suck it all up.
You have been waiting long enough.

FOR THIS, YOU NEED A MAP

Outside, pigeons huddle under eaves too shallow
for any other bird. You hear them at night,
breathing into their closed wings, their collective
murmur a rhythm that radiates through siding and walls.

Beyond the sour cherry trees, the tankers
speed toward the mountain highway
and you think about where else you might go from here.
North to the cliffs. East to the valley. South to the river.

West to where the action is.

You have been planning escapes your whole life,
spending long nights wrapped in blankets with a notebook,
making lists of provisions and destinations, the phone numbers
you want to take with you, studying maps of unfamiliar roads.

This is what you have closed the bedroom door to hide.
Your dog knows but she hasn't revealed your secrets yet.

✳

During the day, you drink coffee, listen to the radio,
walk to the dry cleaners. In the sunshine,
no one can see you scanning the roads, looking
for a path, hidden or otherwise, out.

The bridge is to the right, the cold,
choppy inlet below. It's there you always turn.

You imagine standing midway, leaning into the wind
that blows northeast through Indian Arm, to Belcarra and Anmore,
places you love for the ice-sharp air, for the green moss,
for the nurse logs with which you silently feel a kinship.

The cars driving past would drown out anything
you might say, and no one would ever find anything
you might drop over the barricade. A necklace. A book.
That dress, balled and knotted so it falls with the right velocity.

Every gift. Every last fucking one.

You could be lighter, a bird-bone of a woman.
The sort who would be carried by wind and storm, descending
slowly in circles, until your feet skimmed the surface
and you would submerge, ankles first and head last.

Not sinking, but soaking in salt water until
you're the colour of the night sky reflected in the night ocean.

*

This is the plan. It always has been.
Just under the surface,
the waves obscure your face just so
until there is nothing left to find.

PART THREE

DETRITUS

In your son's pockets, you find the following:

> maple leaves, dried
> pebbles from the schoolyard
> a dove feather
> a plastic sapphire, *Fallen*,
> he whispers, *from the queen's crown*

What you never talk about:

> the glitter he once collected
> from the basement of your last house,
> spilled across the concrete floor
> from a box of loose Christmas ornaments
> you dropped in your hurry to decorate
> a living room you knew you would soon leave

> then, he had swept the sparkly dust
> into an egg cup with his chubby hands
> and placed it on the mantel, the same mantel
> you would punch during a fight that sparked a fire
> in your chest that burned through the sinews
> in your shoulders and arms until your knuckles
> hit the stained oak and you were left
> with swollen hands until New Year's Eve

> maybe the champagne fixed everything,
> but you know that's not true

> your chest aches when you think of that house
> the tall ceilings, the plaster walls, cool to the touch

the egg cup sits on a shelf
in your son's new room
dusty now, behind a pile
of ball caps
if he ever looks at it, he doesn't say

BUT IT PROTECTS YOU FROM THE FIRE
for Andrea

Yes, it's a hard shell but fine
and thin, impenetrable, at least,
for now. It's two years old, polished
smooth by the smoky summer
wind that smells sweet and chemical
from the wildfire burning to the northeast.

    (Four months ago you stood
    on a hill and felt the late winter
    wind on the backs of your legs,
    a push that could have tipped

    you over the edge if you
    were easily surprised. You squinted
    toward the lake, at the low bush
    and birds that flew only inches
    above the ground. You didn't know

    then that a fire would start
    just over there, that where you stood
    was the spot people would stand
    in the August sun and gauge

    how quickly the flames might lick
    and spit toward town.
    There were no signs then,
    but there never are.)

In the night, you listen to the same
song on repeat, the one with a beat
that feels like a kitten heart, nested
in your pocket, small but insistent.
It's an illusion, the softness
of that beat, the fluidity of the bass,
as if your inner softness is visible

and maybe even touchable
by the right person if he asks nicely.
The man rapping says he wants a wife.
He says it so easily and you believe,
for three minutes, that this is the wish
of every man, or at least the one
who hasn't come back to you yet.

You place four different outfits
on the bed for tomorrow. Any
of them will do but you deliberate
anyway. You put away the peasant
top with the sheer sleeves,
the Mary Janes with the inverse heel.
What about the red leather pants?
Yes, always those.

The shell is lacquer, inflexible
and shiny in the right light. One day,
it will crack – in the fall rain
when you swell from the inside
out, or maybe when your mother

finally speaks to you again – but for now
this is what keeps you intact. You look
like a woman with form and purpose,
one who could throw a grenade
into an innocent crowd
without feeling a thing.

SUBTEXT

I

Remember when you secretly passed
your fingers over his eyelashes
while he slept, the tickle on your skin
like the beginnings of love,
if you had to describe it that way.

2

You fold gauze into a bandage for your crying child.
You build a trellis of fallen twigs for pea shoots.
You brush your dog's teeth, black tartar ringing
her gums and you will stall her death
by days or hours or minutes. Whatever you can get.

3

When you were seven, your mother tied
you to the kitchen chair with baker's twine.
You sat for three hours, your ankles and left
wrist swelling around the double knots,
until you, choking but not crying, finished
your congealing dinner.

In class the next morning, you wrote about
a little girl who overpowers a witch
and bakes her unconscious, wart-covered body
in a giant casserole dish. You read it out loud, standing
in front of the chalkboard, and you pulled your sleeve
over your hand, now raw and purple, ringed with one red line
that could have been a friendship bracelet but wasn't.

4

When he comes back to you, his eyes
will roam your face, your stone-still face,
looking for sadness or rage or the dreamy slack of love.

You will allow him one moment of uncertainty
before you kiss him for the first time in months.

You will feel his chest heave, a half-sob or maybe
a release of the old breath he has been saving like a memory.
This is how you know he will not leave you again.

There is always a real story.

THIS IS HOW YOU ANSWER HER
for Carrie

What you didn't know: platelets separated
from the blood are not red or clear
but a deep yellow, thick in the intravenous bag,
Like tangible sunshine, you say, trying
to sound positive but really they terrify
you, their colour like death made liquid,
dripping slowly into the hole the surgeon
has drilled into her chest, her beautiful chest
with the pair of doves tattooed in midflight.

What you have always known: the edge
of her gaze when she asked you the hard questions –
*Do you believe in love anymore, why haven't you
fucked him yet, when will you write the poems again* –
like a scythe to the overgrowth in your head
and then you were quiet until she bought you
another coffee so you would talk and she said,
The world needs your poems, and you laughed
but you believed it too.

What you wish for: her early morning texts
from gas stations in Montana or Wyoming
where her kids are smeared with mud,
their eyes bright because momentum
is what they live for, because speeding
through unfamiliar landscapes is how
she has taught them to calm a restless mind,
because the long unpredictable road, not
the hospital hallway she is now pacing
in mad laps, is the right place for her to be.

DOG YEARS
for Molly

She snored in the night, when you were alone
together, lying on her back, four paws in the air.
It was always a half-whinny and you thought
she might have been dreaming about racing
against a horse on cold sand. She loved the beach
in winter. She loved the wind, sharp salt water
needling her fur and it only made her run faster.
She loved the kelp bulbs that popped in her mouth.

All that sand on the pads of her feet, perfect
for racing dream horses or pretend day horses
or even the seagulls that dipped so low.

You haven't given away her bed or her food
or looked through her bin of abandoned bones.
The brown streak she smeared on the north wall
of your stairwell is still there, two feet high.
You sniffed it today, and it smelled like rain-
soaked fur, like the clumps of mud
you used to wipe from her belly.

But there was no judging her speed. She ran
as fast as she could or she didn't run at all.
She was fast or she was still and nothing in between.
Soon didn't exist. It was, and is, only now.

CHIAROSCURO

The circles under her eyes are purple, fading to yellow
at the edges. *Look what he's done to me*, she whispers.
In old houses, voices carry. Her children – inside
because of this December storm, their ears

already attuned to sadness – could be rooms
away or just around a corner, hidden
by an antique hutch, the grandfather clock
that no one has remembered to wind.

She shows you photos, images he saved.
What is that, you ask. But when you squint,
the blurred pixels clear. A drug you cannot identify.
Porn – bought, made, maybe sold. And then the texts.

    Behind the curtains, you hear
    your son and her son, pretending to be spies, whispering.

How do you get through trauma like this, she says. Her voice
travels flatly and this isn't a question. She pulls
at the ends of hair, now so thin after months
of skipped breakfasts, handfuls of candy at red lights.

    You just do. You have no choice.
    What a bullshit answer that is.

If you asked, would she remember
that time the little boys ran across her yard
naked, tumbled into the trampoline
and shouted to the late summer sky in feral joy?

You had both been drinking rosé
since noon and there was a smudge
of orange smoke below the clouds,
trails of wildfire from the interior.

The boys stopped, exhausted, and lay on their backs,
tracking the stained clouds with their eyes. Your feet
were warm in the sunshine. She leaned against a pillar
on her front porch and her face was planes of light and dark.

    Chiaroscuro, you thought but did not say.

Tonight, her knees are drawn up to her chest
and she lowers her head until you can't see her face,
just her hair, her body caved in on itself. Her shoulders
shake, rising and falling under her pilly grey sweatshirt.

    You do not touch her. She isn't
    that kind of friend. But you say, in a hush, *I know. I know.*

Her daughter, almost eleven, is upstairs, and maybe
she can feel her mother's feelings through the plaster walls
and hollow ceilings. Maybe the cat is with her, warm
and furry, grey on her pink patchwork quilt.

Outside, the winter rain rages against
the single-paned windows. The boys duck
behind the couch and crawl past on all fours
and you both pretend you don't see.

ANATOMY

You have often said, *I bruise easily*, like an apology for the blooms
of blue and purple that will appear on your knees when you trip,
or your hips whenever you bump the footboard of your bed.

If a man touches you, he leaves a mark, sometimes red, sometimes
black. There is no colour logic. Your forty-pound
child-body was tough. Your skin showed nothing.

Not the shoe print. Not the palm on your face. Not the heat rash
from being locked in the station wagon on an August afternoon.
But underneath? Your blood rushed and pooled

in the tender spots, waiting for you to grow up, for your skin
to stretch over a taller body, pulling tight and thin enough
to see through. At eight, you knew never to cry.

At fourteen, you wrote furious poems. At twenty, you turned
to a wall in the emergency room and answered no questions.
At thirty-nine, you wept and he didn't even listen.

You press down on your thigh. It was the birth of your son,
wasn't it, that made you this soft? Those stretch marks, the dip
of your hips when you walk. When a mother cries

in a coffee commercial, you cry too. When a child falls off his bike
on the seawall, you run to catch him, your arms cupped around
his head, a nest. All anyone has to do is look and the signs are there:

cysts on your eyelids, broken capillaries where a mosquito bite once
swelled beyond reason, a cracked nipple. Now, your body shows itself
from underneath every time, the blood that clotted at eight,

fourteen, twenty and thirty-nine ready to liquefy again and make
bruises that seem new but aren't. On your neck, an outline, pink
and red, that matches his hands but you know the shape is only his.

They're just the old hurts, brought to life by the weight
of his upper body on your throat. *Don't worry*, you say again, *I bruise
easily.* He doesn't seem worried and you are half-relieved,

half-tired of anticipating someone else's guilt when there is none.
In the morning, the shower is turned as hot as it can go
and you wince under the water. The towel is rough but so?

When the steam clears, you turn to look in the mirror
and the light over the vanity hides nothing. Do you see that?
You may as well have no skin at all.

POLL

Is it okay to:

want things

stand at a window and wait
    for a man to shatter it with a rock

take a stress nap every afternoon

eat

buy fancy underwear
    and put them in the dryer

not know the answer

listen in the night for heavy feet on your stairs

STIGMATA

You have the mark of a witch.

Turn your palms up. Look closely at the middle.
There: a star, a stigmata from a past life
when you were thrown into a winter-cold river, left
to sink if you were merely human, dragged out
and hung for evil if you floated. The rapids
were vicious, yet in your fists were sprigs of rosemary
that you tore from the bush as the men carried you
out of your cottage and through the garden.

For memory, you thought.
So they will not forget their shame.

As you drowned, the jagged, woody ends
pierced the skin on your palms and you
saw the blood swirl upward to the surface.

White swells, red wisps that spun
like baby hair and then were gone.

✶

You listen to the woman
who claims she has the sight.
She asks, *Are you a conjurer?*
And you say, to your surprise, *Yes.*

There were the imagined men you wrote into poems
who then became real. There was the restlessness
you wrote into your novel and when your marriage
died you wondered what you had called into being.

There is your father, your grandfather
and especially your grandmother. Once,
well past midnight, you opened your eyes
and the neighbour's porch light
spilled over the edge of the bed. It was here
your grandmother sat, perched like a gargoyle
slowly coming to life. By then, she
had been dead for twenty-five years.

She said, *They never knew me. They thought I was cruel.*
Silent, you watched her cry transparent tears.
You wondered if you should touch her,
but you knew that your hand would open and close
and grasp nothing at all. In the morning,
you couldn't remember how she had left.
Maybe she walked.
Maybe she faded away.
Maybe she kissed your forehead
before flying out the window, nimble and weightless.

✻

Cradling your hands in her lap,
the seer asks another question.
Do you get everything you want?
You hesitate.

No. But yes.
She looks at your face, eyes following
the lines of your mouth, set hard in your jaw.
Did he hurt you? Does he scare you?
And you don't bother answering
because you both already know.
He hurt you many times, on purpose
and by accident. The intent never mattered.

You resolve to write a poem that wishes him away,
a place where the desert grows truncated pine trees,
bushes that are grey-green against the dust rising
every time a car passes on the two-lane highway.

He'd like it there. As far
as the eye can see, he will be the tallest one.

In the cramped living room, her three-year-old
dancing to a cartoon on the television behind you,
she traces your lifeline with her fingernail.
So many slashes. Here and here.
She takes a sip of water and then,
Were you a child? What happened?
Before you can reply, she whispers, *I'm so sorry.*

She turns your hand to the side.
There is another marriage in your future.
She smiles.

This time you will be happy. He has been waiting for you.

Someone is smoking weed in an upstairs bedroom
and you blink against the smell.
Well, you say, *where can I find this man?*
She passes you a slice of apple, taken
from a plastic container
shaped like a bunny's head, and laughs.
You're the witch. You tell me.

ACKNOWLEDGEMENTS

To Paul Vermeersch, Noelle Allen and everyone at Buckrider Books for giving me the opportunity.

To Carolyn Swayze, for always being on my side. And to Samantha Haywood for riding with me into the future.

To Andrea MacPherson, Dina Del Bucchia and Shawn Krause for reading drafts of these poems and offering good feedback with the kindest of hearts.

To the Canada Council for the Arts and British Columbia Arts Council for funding the writing of this book.

To Jeff Pohl, for believing in my brain even when I did not, and for loving me even when I really, truly did not.

As always, to Oscar and Rosie, for lovingly reminding me that writing isn't everything.

Earlier versions of some poems have been published in the following: *Making Room: Forty Years of Room Magazine*; *Room* 39, no. 2; *The New Quarterly* 143 and *Poetry is Dead* 17.

JEN SOOKFONG LEE was born and raised in Vancouver's East Side, and she now lives with her son in North Burnaby. Her books include *The Conjoined*, nominated for the International Dublin Literary Award and a finalist for the Ethel Wilson Fiction Prize; *The Better Mother*, a finalist for the City of Vancouver Book Award; *The End of East*; *Gentlemen of the Shade*, *Chinese New Year* and *Finding Home*. Jen teaches at The Writers' Studio Online with Simon Fraser University, edits fiction and non-fiction for ECW Press and co-hosts the literary podcast *Can't Lit*.